Dedicated to the Almighty God and to my parents,
HRH Igwe Charles Okechukwu Nwokedi, Uthoko IV
of Achalla (deceased), and HRH Victoria Amuche
Nwokedi, Etim Eze Azu. —UCU

For John, Robin, and Oliver, with love. —JC

First paperback edition published in 2005
by Chronicle Books LLC.

Text © 2000 by Uzoamaka Unobagha.
Illustrations © 2000 by Julia Cairns.

Book design by Lucy Nielsen.
Typeset in Sabon Oldstyle and Etruscan.
The illustrations in this book were rendered
in watercolor.
Manufactured in Hong Kong.
ISBN 0-8118-5101-x

Library of Congress Cataloging-in-Publication Data
for the previous edition is available.

Distributed in Canada by Raincoast Books
9050 Shaughnessy Street
Vancouver, British Columbia V6P 6E5

10 9 8 7 6 5 4 3 2 1

Chronicle Books LLC
85 Second Street
San Francisco, California 94105

www.chroniclekids.com

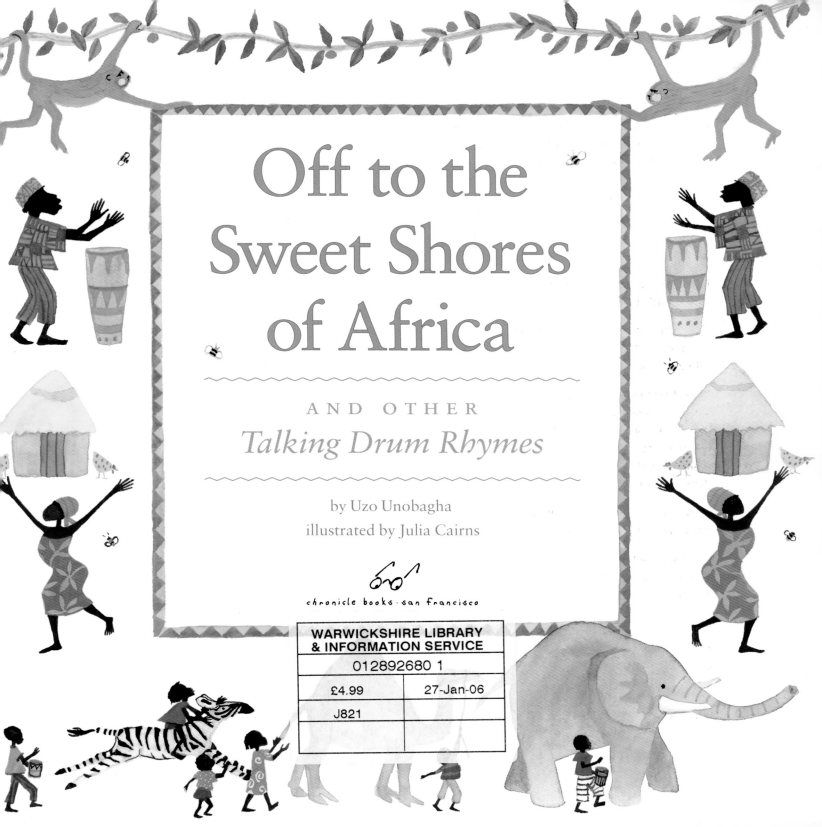

Off to the Sweet Shores of Africa

AND OTHER

Talking Drum Rhymes

by Uzo Unobagha

illustrated by Julia Cairns

chronicle books·san francisco

AUTHOR'S NOTE

The "talking" drum has great significance in West African culture. Once upon a time, many villages possessed a special drum, which was beaten by a person called the crier and was used to deliver the chief's messages to the villagers and the surrounding villages. The people therefore referred to the drum's beat as "talking."

Off to the Sweet Shores of Africa and Other Talking Drum Rhymes is a fitting name for this collection, as it delivers important cultural messages to readers. These rhymes were inspired by my rich cultural heritage. They were also influenced by traditional Mother Goose rhymes which, though not reflecting my cultural experiences, indelibly enchant me and introduced me to the ingenious ability of simple rhymes to present and preserve a culture, from one generation to the next.

Like Mother Goose rhymes, these rhymes embody simple, rhythmic language perfect for young children and beginning readers. And, like classic nursery rhymes, these verses are inhabited by a host of charming characters—Ola Pangolin, the Queen of the Fish, a giraffe named Wobbly Obi, Pineapple Girl and Coconut Boy—and animals both known and novel to literature—impalas, antelopes, cattle, camels, nightjars, sunbirds and fireflies, to name a few.

Unlike Mother Goose rhymes, which present Western ideas and images, these rhymes are quintessentially African. They feature African objects—cowrie shells and akara balls; they evoke the seasons—harmattan and rain; they celebrate the unique African flora and fauna—fields of palm and paprika, coral and mango trees—and offer a wealth of African names and places—from Sahara to Zambezi. Finally, the rhymes reflect distinctly African social mores and themes, like the traditions of telling folktales around firelight and playing by the light of the moon.

I originally wrote these verses for my own children, Ikechukwu and Chukwunonyelum. I wanted them to know Africa, to be transported to the country of their ancestors by the cadence and color of these rhymes. It is my hope that *Off to the Sweet Shores of Africa and Other Talking Drum Rhymes* will inspire readers of African descent to be instilled with not only pride in their culture but with the sheer delight of language, and that for readers of non–African descent these rhymes will introduce Africa and, simply, enchant them. Now, off we go to the sweet shores of Africa!

Uzo Unobagha

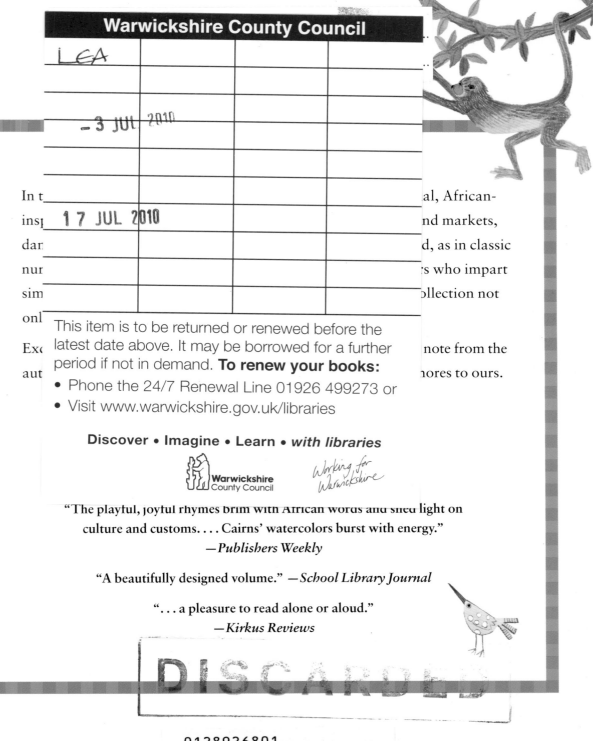

In t_____al, African-
insp_____nd markets,
dan_____d, as in classic
nur_____s who impart
sim_____ollection not
onl____

Ex_____note from the
aut_____nores to ours.

"The playful, joyful rhymes brim with African words and shed light on
culture and customs. . . . Cairns' watercolors burst with energy."
—*Publishers Weekly*

"A beautifully designed volume." —*School Library Journal*

". . . a pleasure to read alone or aloud."
—*Kirkus Reviews*

Off to the sweet shores of Africa,
Off, with my harp and harmonica,
I'll follow the walking, talking drum
To the land, where sunbirds hum.

Off to the sweet shores of Africa,
To fields of palm and paprika,
I'll watch the kingly eagle fly
Beneath the clear blue sky.

Off to the sweet shores of Africa,
Off, in my jar of tapioca,
I'll ride on the River Nile's rolling crest
Till my jar comes to rest.

Ti-Gi-Boom!

Ti-Gi-Boom!

Ti-Gi-Boom!

Ti-Gi-Boom!

Down the baobab went the hare.

Chi-Ki-Boom!

Chi-Ki-Boom!

Chi-Ki-Boom!

Chi-Ki-Boom!

Up he came with a magic pear.

The elephants are trumpeting
All around the town,
Their long, grey trunks are swinging
Up in the air and down.
Let's hurry up and join the parade.
Let's march along the masquerade.
We'll beat our drums and the old ging-gong!
And we'll sing a merry song!

Toodle-loo! Toodle-lei!
My water pot is made of clay;
Woodle-loo! Woodle-lei!
It never has a word to say;
Toodle-loo! Toodle-lei!
Once I went to the square to play;
Woodle-loo! Woodle-lei!
My water pot in a corner, lay;
Toodle-loo! Toodle-lei!
When I came back into the house,
Woodle-loo! Woodle-lei!
It was singing with the mouse!

Ifidom the village drum
Rolled around on his tummy-tum;
He gave his tummy a shake, shake, shake,
And gave himself an ache, ache, ache.

Boom! Boom! Boom-bi-boom!
The drum is marching around the room.
Doom! Doom! Doom-di-doom!
The clay pot is dancing with Bimbo the broom.
Goom! Goom! Goom-gi-goom!
The golden gong is wearing a plume.

Kenechukwu Canary
Perched upon my coral tree.
When I turned and looked his way,
Kenechukwu flew away.

Kenechukwu Canary,
Please don't fly away from me.
I have sat here all day long,
Waiting for your trilling song.

Round and round the mango tree,
Who did run but little me,
With ten bananas in my pail
And ten red monkeys at my tail!

The monkey swings from tree to tree
And hangs by its tail;
The fishes swim from sea to sea
And sometimes in my pail.

"Chirp! Chirp!" calls the cricket,
From his musty, dusty thicket,
"Boys and girls run away to your beds,
The spirits are walking about on their heads."

A-bin-a-pin-a rickety tin,
Is Ola Pangolin in?
She must be in!
She must be in!
She's making such a rackety din!

Nina-Nena-Nelo
Caught a fish by its prickly fin.
The fish made such a frightful din,
That Nina-Nena let it go.

On the muddy bank of the Zambezi,
Danced the Queen of the Fish;
She danced until she was dizzy
And fell right into my dish.

One, two, three, four, five,
Five bees buzzing in their hive;
Six, seven, eight, nine, ten,
Ten chicks hatching in their pen.

A rooster!
A rooster!
Is up on the rafter.
Coo-ka-roo-koo!
Coo-ka-roo-koo!
He is crowing with laughter.

The naughty goat has opened the latch,
With his hippety-hoppity hoof;
Now, he is sitting upon my thatch,
Upon my thatchy, thatched roof.

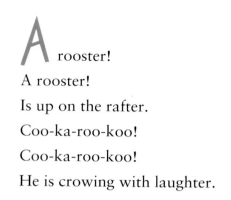

Wobbly Obi, my giraffe,
Has a long and dappled neck.
When he swings it very low,
He can see the smallest speck.
When he swings it up so high,
It is almost in the sky.

When the lions come to play,
The little boys stay away,
The little girls hide by the wall
And do not venture out at all.

"WHERE is old tortoise?" asked Mahmed, "I do not see his limbs and head."

"He's hiding in the basket," said the cricket;

"He's riding on the donkey," said the monkey;

"He's under the mat," said the cane rat;

"He's hanging from a rope," said the antelope;

"He's travelled to Onitsha," said the kingfisher;

"He's playing with the ant," said the elephant;

"I heard him laugh," said the giraffe;

"He's up to a trick," said the dik-dik;

"Oh no! He's not!" said the jumping mouse,

"He's fast asleep in his tortoise-shell house!"

Race the striped zebra across the plains,
Race the striped zebra over the lanes,
Hip! For the zebra!
Hip! For me!
Hurray! For the happy and free!

We're marching across the desert sands,
We're marching away to distant lands,
Crinch! Crunch! Crinch! Crunch!
At night we sing and clap our hands,
And stamp our feet on the golden sands.

Drinking, drinking
From the oasis,
Thirsty camels from distant places;

Kneeling, kneeling
By the oasis,
They rest and watch their tired faces.

Down along the camel's hump,
We like to slide, with feet astride;
Down, we fall with a thumpy thump!
Hurray! For a humpy, thumpy ride!

High above the elephant grass,
Jumps the swift impala,
Sailing past the birds that pass
Above the wide savanna.

High above the grass he jumps,
With a swift and sweeping leap,
Right across the cattle humps
And across the sheep.

H amza Mamza, cattleboy,
Roams from north to south,
Skipping now and then in joy
And whistling from his mouth.

Whistling at the bobbing birds,
Whistling at the bees,
Whistling at the cattle herds,
Dawdling by the trees.

Harmattan is in the air,
Leaves are flopping everywhere.
Here, they flop,
There, they flop,
Birds atop them go hop, hop.

The whirlwind is whirling and swirling around,
Things will be lost and things will be found.
The chickens are scurrying to and fro,
The old man is hurrying along with his hoe.

Up the iroko
Went the wind,
Up and away to Morocco.
Down with the sirocco,
Down it came,
Singing: "Wo! Ho! Ho!"

"Rush!" says the tradewind,
"Rush! Rush! Rush!"
  As it races through the leaves;
"Gush!" says the river,
"Gush! Gush! Gush!"
  As, along its path, it weaves;
"Hush!" says mama,
"Hush! Hush! Hush!"
  As I sleep beneath the eaves.

I'll sweep you along!
I'll sweep you along!
I'm sweeping left and sweeping right,
I'll sweep you along if you don't hold tight!
'Tis the river's rushing song.

Drip! Drop! Plip! Plop!
The gallant rains are marching by.
They will march by every crop
And make them grow twenty miles high.

Rainmaker! Rainmaker!
Make me some rain,
Make it fall on my sugarcane,
Then, they will grow
In a long, pretty row,
Next, I'll cut them all down
And sell them in town.

Rainbow bright! Rainbow bright!
Rainbow arch across my farm!
Rainbow stop! Rainbow drop!
Rainbow hop unto my palm!

When the sun comes out to play,
On a warm and sunny day,
We skip with joy to the village square
And play without a care.

Bomboy blew his bamboo flute,
Round and round the village square;
The children heard his merry toot
And came out leaping in the air;
Hootie-tootie-bom-bamboo!
Bomboy blew his bamboo flute;
Hootie-toot! Greetings to you!
Bomboy blew his merry flute.

I'm off to the market to sell my yam,
I'm off to the market to sell my yam,
I'm off to the market to sell my yam,
My big, brown yam,
From my little farm.

I'll sell my yam for one cowrie shell,
I'll sell my yam for one cowrie shell,
I'll sell my yam for one cowrie shell,
A piece of cloth,
And a silver bell.

Sugarcane! Sugarcane!
Sugarcane sticks!
Buy one stick and you'll get six!
Eat them all
And you'll grow tall!
Taller than all my sugarcane sticks!

Akara ball,
Akara ball,
Taste just one
And you'll buy all.

Yam is yummy,
Yam is yammy,
Yam is yum-yummy
When it's in my tummy.

Grandma makes me plantain flakes,
Grandma bakes me plantain cakes,
Plantain flakes and plantain cakes,
All day Grandma makes and bakes.

Little Pompom drink your pap,
Drink it up while it is hot,
Then, you may have a nappy-nap
On your raffia matty-mat.

Ramadan! Hamadan! Here I come!
With my spoon, and cup, and plate,
With Abdul, my hungry chum,
Ramadan! Hamadan! Don't be late!

Oranges and tangerines,
Their keepers well may frown,
When the boys climb up the trees,
They all come tumbling down.

Pineapple and mango juice,
Pour some into a gourdy cup,
When the girls come back from school,
They will drink it up.

Mouka-Piney, Pineapple Girl,
Dance for me, the pineapple twirl,
Dip and skip, bubble and bounce,
Show the birds your yellow flounce.

Corn rows on my bed,
Corn rows on my head,
Corn rows by the village square,
Corn rows everywhere.

Round and round
My wrapper wraps,
Round and round
My tiny waist,
Round and round
She flaps and laps,
When I'm in a mighty haste.

"Kokori, Kokori,
Coconut Boy,
Give me some milk
And I'll dance in joy."

"A cowrie, a cowrie,
Is all you need;
Give me a cowrie
And dance indeed."

Clicking, clicking, round my ankles,
Are my bonny cowrie shells.
Clicking are my coral bangles,
Clickle-lick, like coral bells.

Clicking, clicking, I'll go dancing,
By the pale light of the moon.
Clicking, back I shall go, prancing
By the bright light of noon.

Let's marry on the Limpopo,
Let's marry under the moon.
Let's sing along the ho! ho! ho!
Let's dance until it's noon.

Let's dance upon the Limpopo,
Let's dance by the light of the moon.
Let's prance to the tune of ho! ho! ho!
Let's prance indeed till noon.

Here we go dancing the rumba dance,
The rumba dance, the rumba dance,
Here we go dancing the rumba dance,
All the way to Port-au-Prince.

The moon is smiling upon my hut
Upon my hut and me;
It's smiling too, on the coconut
On the coconut, up in its tree.

What is the pale moon made of?
What is the pale moon made of?
Of cowrie shells and ivory
Dipped in the shimmering, silver sea
And tossed up like a rubber ball
To be gazed upon by all.

Alight! Alight!
Fireflies alight!
They light up the night
With their bodies abright,
They dance in rings
As the nightjar sings.

Grandpa! Grandpa!
Tell us a tale!
The fire burns brightly,
The moonlight is pale.
We'll sit in a ring,
We'll clap and sing,
Till the pale moon is gone
And your tale is done.

Little boy brown
Where is your papa?"
"He's gone to Congo
To buy me a snail."

"Little boy brown
Where is your mama?"
"She's gone to fetch water
In her nice, new pail."

On Mama's back,
I'm riding high,
I'm riding high,
I'm riding high.

On Mama's back,
I'm riding high,
As twittering birds
Go fluttering by.

Mama hold my little hand,
Mama hold my little hand,
Mama hold my little hand,
As I skip across the sand.

GLOSSARY

In this collection you will find many things unique to West African culture. Below is a list of definitions of the more unusual names, objects and concepts found in the rhymes (in alphabetical order):

Akara ball is a favorite food among children. It is made from ground black-eyed peas (called white beans in West Africa) and is fried in hot oil until it is golden brown.

The **baobab** is a tree featured in many folktales. It is believed to have magical properties and to harbor the spirits of

Bimbo is a female name among the Yoruba people of Western Nigeria.

Bomboy is a pet name given by parents to a son they are fond of.

The **camel** is used for rural transportation and at ceremonial occasions.

Cattle, found throughout Africa, have a hump on their backs.

Chi-ki (Chee-kee)-**boom** is the sound of another popular musical instrument called the Itchaka among the Igbo people of Southeastern Nigeria.

Congo is a country in West Africa known for its large edible snails called Congo meat.

Corn rows is a common hairstyle, which consists of rows of braids lying close to the scalp, resembling rows of corn.

Cowrie shells were used as money long ago. Jewelry made from cowrie shells and coral are worn at traditional ceremonies.

Elephant grass is very tall (up to 6 feet) and is found in the savanna regions of Africa.

At twilight, village children gather under the stars, by an open **fire**, and listen to **folktales** told by their grandparents or other elders.

Hamza is a common Muslim name among the Hausa-Fulani people of Northern Nigeria. Cattle herdsmen and cattleboys from this ethnic group continually drive their cattle from Northern to Southern Nigeria, and back again, in search of fresh pasture.

The dry, windy **harmattan** season lasts from November to February.

The **impala** is a very swift animal that is related to the deer.

The **iroko** is a tree that grows as high as 150 feet. It is common in folktales, as it is believed to possess a spirit that haunts people at high noon and at midnight and that protects animals from hunters.

Kenechukwu (Kay-nay-choo-quoo) is a male name among the Igbo people and means "thank God."

Kokori (Koh-koh-ree) is a boy's name from Southeastern Nigeria.

The **Limpopo** is one of Southern Africa's prominent rivers.

During the full **moon**, when villages of old had no electricity, people gathered at the village square to play, talk, sing and dance, tell folktales and bask in the moonlight.

Mouka is a female name among the Igbo people. Its full form is Moukaosolu (Moo-kah-or-sor-loo), which means "she is older than me."

The **nightjar** is a nocturnal bird.

The **Nile** river is the longest river in Africa.

An **oasis** is a body of water found in deserts, such as the Sahara. It is usually shaded by palm trees. Camels and travelers journeying through a desert stop at an oasis to drink and rest.

Obi is a boy's name, meaning "father's position" or "father's place," among the Igbo people.

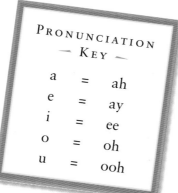

PRONUNCIATION
— KEY —

a	=	ah
e	=	ay
i	=	ee
o	=	oh
u	=	ooh

Ola, short for Olaedo (Oh-lar-ay-doh), is a female name among the Igbo people and means "gold."

A **pangolin** is a small, scaly mammal that looks like a tiny dinosaur. It has been known to strangle a leopard with its long powerful tail.

Pap is a popular food with a yogurt-like consistency made from the cassava crop, which is a root tuber that is similar to the yam and sweet potato.

Plantains are similar to bananas. Plantain flakes and cakes are popular delicacies.

Port-au-Prince is the capital of Haiti, a Caribbean country settled by slaves.

Rain is very important to farming in Africa, especially in the regions that lie near the Sahara Desert. The rainy season lasts from March to October.

A **rainmaker** is believed to possess the ancient meteorological art of holding back the rain for festive occasions, which are usually held outdoors, or making the rain fall, as is necessary for agriculture. The secret of this art is jealously guarded and passed down through generations of rainmaking families.

Ramadan is the most important Muslim festival. It lasts an entire month. During Ramadan, Muslims fast all day and eat only at sunset. It is not uncommon for Muslims to carry eating utensils during this time, for, as soon as the sun sets, they are usually welcomed to eat in any Muslim household. The festival ends with a feast. Muslims compose a large part of the African population.

The **rumba** is a dance that originated in West Africa and was introduced to Cuba and islands in the West Indies by slaves.

The **Sahara Desert** stretches from the northern area of some West African countries, through Central and North Africa and into the Middle East.

The **sirocco** is a hot, dry, dusty and gusty wind that blows in North Africa.

Traditionally, it is believed, **spirits** of the dead wander around at certain times of the day and may cause harm to those whom they encounter.

Ti-gi (Tee-gee)-**boom** refers to the sound made by the talking drum, which is an integral part of West African cultural celebrations.

Toodle-loo! Toodle-lei!: Traditional waterpots, called udo (oo-doo), are made of clay.

The **tortoise** is one of the most popular characters in the folktales of the Igbo people.

A **wrapper** is a large piece of colorful cloth wrapped around the lower body, like a skirt, and knotted at the waist. It is commonly worn by women.

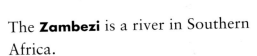

The **Zambezi** is a river in Southern Africa.

Uzo Unobagha was born in Nigeria. She came to the United States in 1995 to join her husband, Ezika. They live in New York with their son, Ikechukwu (Ikey), and daughter, Chukwunonyelum (Noni). This is Unobagha's first children's book published in the United States.

Julia Cairns is a fine artist who lived in Botswana, Africa, for nine years. She now lives in Northern California with her husband, John, and their children, Robin and Oliver. This is her second children's book